Glass
Hat

GLASS HAT

RICHARD STANSBERGER

Louisiana State University Press
Baton Rouge and London
1979

Copyright © 1979 by Richard Stansberger
All rights reserved
Manufactured in the United States of America

Designer: Albert Crochet
Typeface: VIP Palatino
Typesetter: LSU Press
Printer and binder: Thomson-Shore, Inc.

Grateful acknowledgment is made to the editors
of the following, in which several of these poems
have appeared, sometimes in slightly different form:
Archive, Cincinnati Poetry Review, Clifton, Hanging Loose,
Mother Jones, Penny Dreadful, Prospectus, Rainy Day,
Slipshod Review poemcards, *Stardancer, Waters.*
"A Collision Text" appeared in *Cincinnati Poetry Review*
as "Two Collision Texts."

LIBRARY OF CONGRESS CATALOGING IN PUBLICATION DATA

Stansberger, Richard, 1950–
    Glass hat.

    I. Title.
PS3569.T3334G5   811'.5'4   79–12312
ISBN 0-8071-0557-0
ISBN 0-8071-0558-9 pbk.

For Denise Levertov

CONTENTS

ARCANA: POEMS FROM THE TAROT

THE SPARROW OBSESSIONS

for Judith Dunaway

FOR X, WHO KNOWS WHO SHE IS

I can't talk to you here
this poem is bugged
        hear that apostrophe buzzing?
        notice how that verb just got louder?
there is a certain balding young man
with headphones
in some gritty attic or toilet stall
so meet me on the square at noon tomorrow
just stand there by the fountain
I'll be disguised as a gust of fresh air
and I'll signal you
by ruffling the soft hair of your arms

THEM

"I am a man of
unlimited pretensions,"
he told me.

His woman is talented in
making herself small.

At night he is Michelangelo
on his back painting
her ceiling with snores.

She sleeps in his boot.

Once I sat on their back steps
listening for discontent
but the wind rattled the ivy
and it was too cold to stay.

HERE

Here, take this rose. I'm tired of being selfish.
And here, how about this catfish. He does tricks.
Put him in a swimming pool and he pulls off people's suits.
And this glass music, see how it makes rainbows?

O I'm sorry. Your hands are full.

Only children aren't very good at giving things. They're
not trained for it. Well, the catfish can hold some of the stuff
in his mouth, and this snow flurry can just
follow you home. How about this spool of dream. Great
for embroidery on your jeans. When I was little and some kid
gave me candy, it was always because he didn't like that kind.

I know your arms must be tired, but I've been in love with you
for so long. You can put the stuff in this tornado.
Nothing will get hurt. It whirls everything around at the same
speed. Yes, it scared me too, at first, the way it followed me
in dreams until I called it by name. Just tell it to
stand at a distance until you get used to it. Later you can
ride inside if you want to.

This is just an old wheelbarrow, but I want you to have it.
It's the one I used to sit in at Grandpa Pydynkowsky's,
pretending I was birch logs for the stove. If you don't want it,
that's O.K. Just ignore it, and after a while, it'll roll off
to some construction site.

How about this bear. I like bears. And this pig. They're
more fun than dogs or cats, though they cost a little more to feed.

O I forgot how small your house is. Well, we can't put them
in the tornado. I've tried it. The bear just gets sick, and the
pig turns mean.

Why hell.
Take this universe. It's small, but it'll hold everything.
Don't forget to wind up the moon.

BUT NOT

If this were the city, I'd just
find another bar, and
take a different bus to work.

But this globe is smaller, no
ridges or valleys from tectonic
growth, no imperfections
for the snow to hide.

I drive past your place at
least twice a night, your little
house with its contradictory lighting:
one small lamp when you're awake,
and when you sleep the big yellow
bulb over your door is bright,
expectant.

TRESPASS

The moon won't leave this poem.
I pushed it out of the sky
telling it that it was symbolic,
not a moon at all (it was
freezing in my palm).

But here it is again,
like an old lover's face
in a dream.

So, given that you and I
are stuck with this moon up there
full and white as though it never
rose up red out of the
dead trees, looking as though it's
doing us a kindness staying here
at all, as though it's not chained
to earth like the rest of us,
but just floating there, beatific,
with its survivor's scarred face,

So, given that this moon will not
go away, but keeps laying its image
in the river and silvering the rocks,
given that somehow when it shines
the sirens must run all night,
there's not much else to do but
listen to its one sound
its ringing little maniac note.

DECISIONS

whether the milky sun
will produce bird cries
or whether I will follow
dozer treads through the mud

"when I was in love with you"
I said to the sparrow
"you were everything but
a sparrow—a flock of
iridescent grackles   a drop
of blood flying through pines"

"I'm nothing but a sparrow"
said the sparrow   "you
saw what you wanted to see"

but she was wrong   the sun
turned the clouds golden
and the grackles   clanging
burst out of the trees

SHADY GROVE

there are
children
in your
hair

they
stare
at me
solemnly

but
you're
woven
of sun
filtered
through
autumn

I
hold out
my hand

our
children
are dust

they
float
in you

float
and glitter

MAKING FRIENDS
WITH THE DEAD

EMIGRANT

I was born in a constitutional monarchy
where Salvador Dali is president
and nobody knows who is king, where
the money, when they use it at all,
is dried moss. As a child, crazy
from drinking the red honey,
I would be put on a yellow train
and ride singing through the mountains.
In the summer we slept out while
the trees tuned their instruments.
During the day I caught
emerald grasshoppers with red eyes
and held them to the sun.
The girl I love may still be there.
I remember licking her neck and how much
like cream she tasted. On fiesta days
she would hang the phone poles with wind chimes
and watch Sigmund Freud on TV.
I wonder if killers there still
turn into piles of coins, and if
the dead are still buried in pumpkin seeds.
It was the nuns who led me away,
convincing me I was miserable. Oh I would
give my glass hat to go back there.

AUTOBIOGRAPHICAL FOUND

Basil:
Companion to tomatoes;
Dislikes rue intensely.

The Rodale Herb Book
edited by William Hylton

THESE PEOPLE

for Gary

These women were girls
when their fathers died.

This man
listening to the jazz piano
still wonders why
they buried his mother
before he was told.

These people
blur a little
on cloudy days. Half-
moons grow behind their eyes.

We who want them
hold on tight
while they turn into rain.

A COLLISION TEXT

Avoid confusing similar bells
or misusing the principal parts
of footpaths

Use logical oranges in sequence

Use the green mood in the few
types of fruit in which it is
still appropriate

Avoid needless shifts in
moon and sea

Observe such distinctions as
exist between the heart,
oranges, and the full moon

> *Harbrace College Handbook*,
> 7th edition, & a poem by Lorca

WEDNESDAY AFTERNOON

A man walked by me on the street. I was bending to look at a piece of paper with writing on it. He had no shirt on, and there were rubber bands squeezing into the flesh of his arms and neck, and several of the big postal size bands were making creases around his stomach and chest.

The writing on the paper was in pencil, about how a cat praises God by being a cat and how a dog praises God by being a dog. I'd written something like that years ago when I was in third grade, and my teacher, Miss Dee, was so worried (as I later heard) about being pregnant that she couldn't concentrate, and would make us do exercises about the will of God, or make us count the periods in fifty pages of our religion books. It was good discipline, she said.

A man walked by me going the other direction. He was a mailman, and I smiled, because my father is a mailman. I know how it is, you poor bastard, I tried to tell him with my smile, but he just said, Something you want mailed? No.

The handwriting on the piece of paper was childish, of course. There was a tennis shoe mark on the page, and the thing had been folded and unfolded a number of times so that it was soft now, like cloth. I'm always expecting to find a joke planted by God in little happenings like this. Unable to see one here, I put the paper back on the ground, crumpling it up so that it would be less likely to blow away. I'm not one to spoil a joke.

I would have taken the advice on the paper and praised God by being myself, but how can I be anything but myself, I thought, and so walked across the water that was running down the pavement from somewhere out of sight and was falling into a storm drain with a sound like applause. The water licked up over the sides of my sneakers and onto the black cloth and felt good.

There was a creek near our house that ran from a little reservoir down into a series of culverts through the center of town. It always smelled fishy, and both Miss Dee and Mrs. Charles, a doughy old woman who taught fourth grade, had health stories about it. The way I understand it, just stepping into that little creek would cause your feet to swell up with tuberculosis and cause the skin to crack and ooze pus.

It had been awhile since I'd been fishing. Fish were so different from me that it always seemed wrong to kill them. Animals with lidded eyes and fur were somehow O.K. though I'd stopped killing them too because they were much more interesting when they ran away, or killed each other, or snoozed in the sun without even thinking of me, than when they were jerking a bloody hind leg or clawing the grass.

Before getting into my car, which is red, I looked back down the sidewalk. A man pushing a two-wheeled cart full of groceries had stopped to pick up the paper. I saw the green neck of a wine bottle sticking out of the top bag. Once I had dropped a wine bottle on the sidewalk downtown and cut my foot on a piece of green glass later that night in the same spot, even though I had stopped and picked up as much of it as I could find. It had been hot, and my hair kept falling into my eyes as I bent over, and I swore at myself because it had been pretty good wine.

Just as I started the car, a golf cart pulled up alongside, waiting for a light. The man driving it looked like Bob Hope in a red baseball cap, and there was a girl beside him with long frizzy brown hair and a fur coat. She looked very much like a woman I'd seen in a dream, who'd been pregnant, and had delicate brown arms and legs between which were stretched butterfly wings set with clear stones and beads of glass.

But then everything always threatens to become everything else, if you're not careful. She kept looking over at me, but I wasn't in the mood to talk, so I just nodded. The brown stetson on my head suddenly decided (as I figured it would, one of these days) to pretend to be a chicken hawk, and as I pulled away from the curb, it lifted off my head and into the back seat. The golf cart was gone. In the rearview mirror I saw three men banging on the road with the flats of their shovels.

I began to hope that the woman in the fur coat was pregnant, and that the baby was somehow mine, until I remembered that in the dream I had made love to and then become the woman, so that even if the other woman was pregnant, it wouldn't matter, because she'd have to be me, and that was, at this point, impossible.

I was still thinking of jeweled wings as I drove into a supermarket not far away, and of how in the dream even the pellets of the shotgun of one of my old professors had just passed through them as they instantly healed, and of how nice it had been to float among the tall buildings on the waves of exhaust from rush hour traffic. Then a shopping cart rolled in front, and I had to stop quick to keep from hitting it. The afternoon sun made it shine more like cobweb than steel.

Among the things I had decided to buy were eggplant (unless it's too old and going brown, its purple curves are like the curves of space), some red wine, and some Campbell's soup, which I grew up on, and which I love, I realized, because it always tastes the same no matter where you are.

DON'T MAKE FRIENDS WITH THE DEAD

They end up coming over every morning,
with a flicker and pop
as soon as you step into the shower.

Then all day long you follow them around
asking questions like a dumb little brother.

They go from room to room for their own reasons.
Handel loves the soap operas and the way
the silver sounds when he dumps out the drawers.
Gogol is fascinated by the rock collection,
and Otto III studies the scrolls of light
unfolding on the floor.

But the dead bore easily, get blurry, and you
end up following them down the basement stairs
where they disappear through a back wall
and you suddenly notice your bare feet
cold in the dirt of the root cellar.

WHAT IT WAS LIKE

but you don't remember what it was
like

said the bearded man as he went
through
the wallet of the corpse

you were young then, maybe not even
born

as he cut off the pocket watch
I wondered how one with such sad
eyes
could be so deft

KILLBUCK: A POEM FOR GRINDERS

I.
Spitting orange seeds off the loading dock
old Killbuck said:
People ask me if I'm an alcoholic
and I just say
Whyno.

II.
Killbuck stands in a cloud of dust
pressing a steel cylinder to the
screaming stone wheel.
Sweat streaks his face mask.
Sparks pit his leather apron.

III.
Back in 1947 while playing ball
Killbuck noticed he couldn't close his hands.
He showed the plant nurse.
—When did it happen.
  Who are your witnesses.
—Twenty years as a goddam grinder,
  that's when it happened.
—I'm sorry but I need a specific time and place
  and a specific witness or witnesses
  or I can't turn it in for compensation.

IV.
Things I learned from him:
how to shell a boiled egg with a spoon,
how to build a hammock out of crate sides,
when to sneak off and sleep in it,
how to goose guys with the air hose,
how to tell the age of a chainman
        (count his missing fingers),
where to hide the bottle.

CHRIST

And so he had a head of clouds
while others dragged their stone feet
scraping sparks off the ground
and calling it light.

And what happened to him?
Rust and blood like the rest of us.

And what did he say about it?
Much. Though his words are water
and take their shape
from whoever contains them.

THE DISAPPEARING MAN

sat in his woman's bathtub watching the warm water swirl his legs, smelled the cheese omelet frying in the kitchen, heard the sweet wood of recorder music, wished he could stay there forever. And he did.

He watched a red squirrel through his sights while a hawk slammed in and sailed off with it through the yellow leaves. Fog and the sounds of cows. He stayed there, too.

He also stayed forever just waking up on a boulder in Utah while the sun flared the canyon rim and somebody was taking his picture. And forever on a backroad where the moon glistened the tar and clotted leaves, as the crickets sang like they didn't know it was autumn.

I know how it will end, he said to himself. By the railroad tracks a shoe with a foot in it, in a hay loft a small piece of bone, on the floor of a bus station a sleeve with an arm. So that when I finally see the skin of my hand holding to the steering wheel as I drive through some bland little town, disappearing the rest of the way will be a cinch.

SO MUCH

It's not so much being trapped
among those with shaved heads

or breathing the burnt air

as knowing that something
beautiful
has just walked by
on the other side of a thick hedge
going the other way

DINAH SHORE
AT THE FIRST
INTERGALACTIC
MIXER

What
are
you
back
home
?

I
mean
What
do
you
do
?

No
,
not
What
are
you
doing
,
I
know
what
you're
doing
,
I
mean
What
do
you
do
for
a

living
?

O.K.

,
let
me
rephrase
that

,
What
do
you
do
to
or
for
others
of
your
kind
so
that
you
get
what
you
need
to
live
?

I
see

.

.

.

Uh
,
no   .
,
not
with
each
other's
flesh
we
don't
,
not
usually
,
anyway
.
.
.

SO HERE'S MARK putting both feet behind his head while sitting on the couch at Gail's mother's forgetting all he has on is his bathing suit showing the old lady his hairy balls. Here's Mark waving his floppity wrists clapping with one hand announcing to Heather the harpist that now she's Enlightened. And Mark walking through the house of Dr. Somebody during another conservatory party talking about nipples and hanging all the phones up the wrong way. And improvising for an hour at the piano around one of his old themes because something is bothering him too much to talk about and me looking out the window at the campus watching his music change my vision. Mark with Annie. Mark with Terri. Mark with Mary Ann and then Chris and then Shelley. Mark with Sandy and his mother and father at their twenty-fifth anniversary in the rented hall where his mother gets Gordon and Gail and me so drunk we have to stay all night. Then Mark is gone outside the darkness and his music comes through my headphones opening up something golden like that one chord in the Rite of Spring and then windchimes and copper and the tape runs out. Here's that one time when Kathy and I dared him to put all his clothes on backwards and come with us to Frisch's and he got us to do it too. So yesterday a letter came from San Francisco typed in green saying "My hair is getting thin but then who wants fat hair" so here's Mark again but just barely.

AN OPENING AT THE ART CENTER

for Jim Krailler

The tall bony woman in the black leotards came over   "O you must
be the *poets*"   Then Mel from New York with the wraparound shades
made us take off our shoes and walk "feet absolutely flat on the floor;
you know, like Rodin's John the Baptist"   We were supposed to move
in a slow line chanting something like wood wood wood to show the
Indian Hill art patrons how well Bony Woman and Mel had captured
our city's pioneer heritage   After that, in the center of the gallery in a
little circle of light Jim and I sat to read our poems as the patrons
moved back and forth from the open bar   One woman in Bedouin
dress and Navajo silver and her husband in grey leisure suit with
purple neckerchief walked between us as if we were transparent like
the legless man selling papers on Vine Street   Then others were
walking through as well, talking vacation or inviting each other to
parties   Jim started with the explosion in that bar last spring, and I
read the one about the boy they fished out of the lake   I had to watch
his lips sometimes to know when to start reading   Then Jim did the
one about the hermit and I read "State Hospital Sunset" twice because
it was so short   A woman sat down drunk and put a dish of plastic
flowers in front of my toes   When Jim and I ignored her, she put her
feet behind her head so we could see her pink panties   Then Bony
Woman appeared and whispered us off   The black caterer's daughter
had sad eyes and showed us to the kitchen where a Big Mac, half a
cheese, and a bottle of Masson sherry were all that would fit into my
briefcase

CINCINNATI PHONE BOOK POEMS (1976)

I. How to Succeed
590 Powers—Preferred
591 Preferred—Price
592 Price—Princeton
593 Princeton—Profitt

II. Boredom
393 Jones—Jones
394 Jones—Jones
395 Jones—Jones

WHAT I ALWAYS WANTED TO

What I Always Wanted To
is gone. The orchestra
is packing up, the
audience has left, the
hall is as sad
as my father's eyes.

What I Always Wanted To
has left, and I'm looking
across Lake Superior
at Isle Royale green in its fog.

Not that the going was sudden:
the door opened so slowly
the curtains exhaled so slowly
that the kids playing on the floor
didn't even look up.

What I Always Wanted To
has forgotten its own name,
thinks it's fog in love with
the grass.

What I Always Wanted To
is gone. I hear deep breathing
outside the grass is sighing
but here in this room it's cold
and the darkness snickers.

"NO ATHEISTS IN THE DRESSING ROOM"

1. Faith Is a Star
2. Pat Boone

3. He Is Only a Prayer Away
4. John Wayne

5. And a Little Child Shall Lead Them
6. And It Came to Pass
7. Jerry Lewis

8. Gratitude
9. Sammy Davis Junior

10. Thy Will Be Done
11. Ethel Waters

12. Let's Make a Deal
13. In Thy Pure Sight
14. Alan Young

IN A DIFFERENT PITCH

When the couch was brown and the wallpaper was tan
and the carpet was light brown and even the light was tan,
my dead sisters were hiding all the time behind the air.
They had died without names. They were too young to smile.
They just watched us with eyes that forgot to shut. My
dog knew that, I realize now, and would let them
stroke her fur while she slept behind the couch. My father
knew too, and tried to give them room while never letting himself
see what they lived on. My mother tended to her ruined family
as carefully as she smoothed the beds and polished the kitchen floor.
I thought that what touched my head and the hair on my arms as
I played alone was only the air. I still don't know what made
my mother finally give that clipped recitation of why she
always included three oversized angels in the nativity set.
I've finally forgiven her, and forgiven myself for refusing
to be her family all alone. And I've forgiven my sisters too,
even though when I'm visiting there and working late at night,
I can hear them take the sound of the typewriter and
send it back in a different pitch.

SHILOH

(completely from the memoirs of U. S. Grant)

I reassumed command   east bank   crump's landing   pittsburgh
landing   corinth   important railroads   all the cotton states
possession of corinth   railroad   confined to his bed   general
prentiss   general buell   general smith   a line to intrench nearer
the river   even from the creeks   the creeks . all the movements
of the enemy   johnston's   this cavalry   large body of the
enemy   safety of crump's landing   destroy our transports   lew
wallace   much injured   my horse falling   firing was heard
my boot had to be cut off   crutches

general nelson   buell   up the east bank at breakfast   heavy
firing   hurried note   dispatch-boat   under arms crump's
landing   captain baxter   general wallace   colonel mcpherson
captain rowley   wallace did not   crosses owl creek
right of sherman   general wallace   wholly raw   log meeting-house
mcclernand   sherman's left   prentiss stuart   still sick in
bed at savannah hearing our guns   lick creek   owl creek
snake creek   water very high   our line of tents soon fell
into their hands   ground heavily timbered   considerable under-
brush   sherman   the firing   a mile in the rear

flanks   general prentiss   2,200 of his officers and men captured
snake creek   lick creek   heavy firing   muskets
officers broke   cowards   whistle of bullets   bloody   cavalry
could not   stragglers   lying under cover of the river bluff
dispatch-boat   top of the bluff   colonel j.d. webster   more
pieces of artillery   deep ravine   hurlbut   this artilllery
mcclernand   sherman   snake creek   shattered
w.h.l. wallace   heavy fire   gone   snake creek   log-house
sherman   lew wallace

after dark   deep ravine   gunboats the artillery
any of buell's   at least 7,000   night   rain fell in torrents
under a tree   bruise so painful   no rest   log-house
as hospital   night   wounded men   an arm or a leg amputated
unendurable   I returned to my tree in the rain

in the morning   in the camps   the confederates   shells by the
gunboats   every fifteen minutes   wallace   sherman   mcclernand

hurlbut   nelson   crittenden   mccook   battle became
general   all day   in front of myself to prevent premature firing
a clearing   executed with cheers and a run   last enemy broke
while riding toward the river   musketry   shells and balls
whistled upon us   poor beast dropped dead   scabbard of my sword
lying in the mud and rain
several miles   after the battle   enemy had dropped   provisions
extra wheels   field hospital   open field   covered with dead
walk across   stepping on bodies without a foot touching the ground

WHAT THE DIFFERENCE IS

the difference is yellow
wrap it around your head
never cut your hair

the difference is white
drifting over the rocks

the difference is black
the difference stings
those cracks in the sky
are sometimes called trees

FRIENDS

for Jacquie

My friends, the men, some with beards
in their voices the sound
of furniture moved against a door
or the scrape of a blade across a whetstone.

The women, also my friends,
their voices shuffle like rain on the streets
twist into madrigals
like those in the weedstalks.

As I rock back and forth by the stove
my own voice is quiet
a rifle bolt slid slowly back.

CONFESSIONAL POEM FOR HIS
TWENTY-THIRD YEAR

A man born under the sign of Libra
will be able to see all sides at once:
eyes, face, breasts, back, vagina.
He will have some trouble making
decisions. In his mind are tuned medieval bells.
He is polite and somewhat conservative,
with morals the consistency of tapioca.
Librans are long on insight and short on courage.
He will, however, dare to eat a peach,
along with a plum, two apples, a roast duck,
and three chocolate eclairs. Praise his art
and he will spitshine your shoes for life.

ONTOLOGUE

well here we all are
said the sparks
to the black
said space
to vibration

well
here we all are said
flash to sullen
said thick to silent
frozen to burning blue

and here
said the hand
that took the axe
and here said the
bite of the axe to

the bend in the fiber
to the shifting of dirt
to the jostling of rock
to the tilt of the axis
of space around which
something vast and grey
rippled yes hello   yes hello

ARCANA: POEMS FROM THE TAROT

0.
FOLLY

Up in the mountains
looking at the vast,
he runs along a ledge
his white dog behind him.

He is proud of the poems
in his backpack as he is
proud of his backpack and
embroidered shirt.

All that space breathing
makes him want to jump.

He is a spark from the
same fire as the sun.

The dog is yapping
and means to
crowd him off the edge.

I.
DOUBLE HARPSICHORD CONCERTO

In the dark of my closed eyes
Handel
wiser than my mother
covered me with gold brocade

In the cold dark of my closed eyes
Handel smiled
knowing that not to freeze
means to imagine yourself warm

II.
THE MAGICIAN'S DEAD SISTER

when he sleeps
I conjure
him

his
silence

is
what I answer

under
the snow
I am
the seed that holds its breath

III.
THE EMPRESS

he writes me poems all the time
once he told me that in
the dark space between
his hand and my hip
his mind became lost and
whirled away in its shiny suit
till it was just another star

IV.
IMPERATOR

She's fucking around again
but that's O.K., so am I.

One of the houseboys
showed me some of his
poems
for christ sake.

At least he's harmless.

Maybe keep her from
bitching so much.

Now if he ever
writes something like
Lycidas
I'll have to nail his ass.

V.
THE POPE

the pope is speaking from the balcony pigeons
fly out of his eyes when he cleans his glasses
the man on TV is clearly at home the way his
eyes move head swivels voice ignores the fact
we're making a sandwich or reading a book
the pope is walking through his library takes down
a copy of the index of forbidden books the light
from a small casement slides along the floor
there is frost on the inside of the window the man
on TV is explaining why there is no more heat the
pope puts down his coffee looks out the window of
the airplane rows of crosses below seem to wave
the man on TV is interviewing a fat man in a suit
the fat man used to make movies the man on TV asks
him about his pet dogs the pope has just finished
writing about the starvation of millions he puts
his head down on his desk drowsy one of the books
on a shelf behind him hums quietly a struck bell
the hair of the man on TV is longer now and darker
he is telling why we must keep calm he no longer jokes
about the police there is a bulge under his left arm
the pope lies in bed looking at the canopy pulling
the threads apart with his mind the man on TV fails
to appear one day there is another man who resembles
him who makes little jokes about him the pope in the
mirror notices his hands are bone the wire glasses
since he has no nose slide down his face clatter
on the floor someone takes him by a sleeve his
armbones are slung leads him to a door behind a
bookcase the new pope resembles a man on TV several
years ago he takes a letter opener sticks it through
his lower lip a piece of blotter paper to catch
the blood someone is cheering the man on TV has wire
trouble temporarily no one can hear him he panics
his clean wire glasses the pope is drawing
test patterns on his desk

VI.
THE LOVERS
(for two voices
simultaneously)

She:

Joy
is my
shadow
springs
at dawn
from the
soles
of my
feet
expands
at
dusk
becoming
the whole sky

He:

All
the voices
in the
cello
in a
distant room
I love
when you
play
I
sit still
when it starts
I write it
all down

VII.
STRENGTH OF HIS ARMS

he is striding to the blackboard Bishop Sheen is
striding to the blackboard one hand clenched
around chalk he is making one of his little jokes
about the angel who does the erasing he is drawing
an outline human head he is demonstrating the dif-
ference between the inner and the outer man

A man of God is a man of peace

his eyes toll the words glow

He is at peace with all around him

he paces before the camera the air parts his hands are
huge sculptor hands not of the earthly the vainglorious
politician or merchant who impresses
only events

How can this be?

voice rising to the question   there is a close-up of
his face with its bones with its teeth

Because the man of God
                    has crucified

his hand flies to the blackboard chalks furious
crosses into the head his voice soft now satin
over the face

Has crucified the man within!

after the sermon he lifts his arms in benediction
his cape is wings spreading behind him but falls back
while the huge hands rise

VIII.

STRAWBERRIES

*Things rising from the mind
Have no real being. What's real
Is the strawberry. And yet.*
          Shinkichi Takahashi, "Strawberry"

The women are no longer conservative.
Since my great-uncle Frank died
they've refused to do chores,
and the strawberries in the big patch
between the house and the road
are going soft and leaking into the ground.

There are still some to save, and I
eat these on the porch swing
running my toes through the fur
of the lonely collie's back.

The rain comes and softens outlines.
The curtain of hills ripples.
At one time the curtain was proof that I
would first go crazy then shoot myself.
Things rising from the mind have
no real being. And yet.

The garden has become mud between my toes.
The strawberries, near bursting,
are held together by their seeds,
each of the seeds rounded and possible.
Their juice is sticky on my hands.

There is a shuffle in the kitchen
and a small rumble. Florence or maybe Marylin
is pushing the table back to make room
in front of the stove. They are frying
bacon for the dandelion greens.

The spouting on the porch roof leaks.
The rain falls, doing only what's necessary.
These strawberries are nothing like
the tiny ones that grow wild.
And yet they're good, and their stickiness
is good.

If the rain stops.
I'll go look for deer tracks in the hills.

IX.
UNCLE JOHN

Because he hated the patent office
all John Summers' best inventions,
the double windmill, the fancy wagon brake,
the windup electric heart stimulator,
got stolen the moment he showed them.

He sold every rock and weed on his three farms
to feed his lathes and drills.

When he died even his beard broke down.

But his nose lying in a pasturefield
took root. His eyelids floated down
the creek like leaves. The jeweled spiders
from his heart hung their bright yellow webs
all over my grandmother's kitchen.

X.
THE GREAT MACHINE

(Boy Presumed Drowned in Lake
Superior)

the one whose eye is air
sees birches rise white fountains
shoot green leaves that fall to earth yellow

the one whose skin is space
feels layers of brown grass
through which a boulder slowly moves

the one whose mind is sea
drowses under ice or wakes with sun
but cannot suspect among snagging rocks
the crumbling starlike shape

XI.
SO

So out of sorrow and loss and helplessness she drowned herself, and the last thing through the water was his face looking down. He showed no love, only horror, and was gone. She was a bubble in the black and the black suddenly gave way to greenish light. Fish swam by her in the caress of water, big fish, giving her passage, causing no trouble. She forgot her fright in the surprise that she was holding her breath so well, that she had breath to hold at all. The muscles that moved her limbs were joyful, said to her *welcome* and *relax* and *how strong*.

She saw a flash of yellow, duck feet above her, breaking surface. And so she was rising before she knew it, now tasting the water, grasping with her hooked beak the yellow flesh, careful not to break through bone, becoming in her shell a dead weight sinking down, all the time eyes open, until the duck's white thrashing stopped.

Suddenly nervous water. A new disturbance. She rose and looked, feeling her eggs jostle inside her. Huge shapes on the far side in the stinging light, diving in, thrashing the water. Time enough to get that duck later, she thought, heading off toward the cattails.

XII.
SHINKICHI TAKAHASHI

an old man's skin
fell over my face

the sun is dull red
has hollow eyes

if the body is smoke
if the body is smoke
why does the wind
feel so good

XIII.
SUICIDE (10/4/74)

your picture had become
grey dots of pain

last week, Anne, your
hands unclenched

the eyeless black butterflies
swarmed out

XIV.
EYESIGHT

the whitehot steel
left the ladle
hit the wet mold with a
boom   that made me jump

I was twelve
they were pouring light

my uncle who ran the place
watched them as the glow
polished his steel-rim glasses

XV.
THE SHED

light stands in the shed taking into itself the dust. there is a cat and there is a bag of lime split open the lime making a little hillside up the bag. dried onions and the smell of rust. whether the cat is locked in, whether the cat has been locked in for days is not important, the cat is thirsty. chains hang from the wall, there are hatchets and crowbars leaning, there is a blunt sledge a double-bladed ax an adze. whether the cat is thirsty or whether the dust in the air is thirsty and has filtered the cat's dreams, the iron-wheeled lawnmower ticks and creaks by itself smeared with dry grass. the cat is dirty, it has licked its fur and the dust has stuck. the cat is licking wood and steel. under a window is a fat file, the cat is licking it, the cat is beginning to purr, whether the skins of the muskrats tacked to stretchers in the rafters or whether the blunt traps witness this means nothing to the purring to the rising and fall of the cat's ribs to the reddening of its whiskers. this file is juicy this file is surprising. whether or not the cat begins to whimper as it drinks or whether or not its teeth are broken glass, the dust of the floor is becoming dark and there will be plenty more to drink.

XVI.
HERE IN THE SNOW
(note tacked to the last fencepost)

You are entering a new phase in your existence.
You are walking into a long pause between words.
You may as well discard that bag of seeds you carry.
Can you see any place to plant them here? You are
entering a time full of itself, with much to give
you practice in distance. Do not be alarmed if the
snow and grey sky have stolen the horizon, or if all
your steps seem downhill. To find a landmark, you
must contract to ermine size or expand to snowcloud.
Neither of these is superior. You will leave your
boots either for fangs and anger or for helplessness
and freedom from cold. You need not hurry in your
decision. In fact, you may also choose to remain
as you are, if you do not fear being lost. After all,
when you consider it, do you still believe that your
destination was worth all your hurry?

XVII.
STARS

Me and Dan and Bob and Joannie and Sheila and the woods are
giggling and that was before they put up all those lights when the
park was still fun and around us swirled green and black and
magnolia forsythia honeysuckle

The universes were laid on top of each other like paper plates that's
what I was thinking and then Joannie hollered look look and we were
standing on the edge of a vast hole a deep black gap in our universe
cleverly disguised as Burnet Woods Pond   Aha! I thought and said
as much and poor Bob who still looked like Richard Nixon with his
jowls because of the wisdom tooth operation had to be held (Joannie
gladly obliged) to keep from falling through the hole trying to see
what world was stacked below ours

So when Mark came strolling by with his pinstripe self after walking
some girl to her car and we explained it carefully and he made some
crack about drugs, Dan said no really it's all true Mark just look down
there you can see a whole nother bunch of stars

Mark was still scowling and I said but anyway you guys he might not
believe us but that just proves we're right

XVIII.
JUDITH WITH HEAD OF HOLOFERNES

after a painting by Sandro Botticelli

She is walking very slowly with the curved blade, mostly cleaned of blood, still in her right hand. Her eyes are sad but she has not been crying. She is staring off to her right, not conscious of where she is walking. Perhaps she is remembering how it felt when he came inside her. She may still have some of his sperm between her legs. She seems to feel cheated: for one thing, he was surprisingly like any other man—though his skin had a foreign tang—hardly a conqueror, the way he tongued her nipple; for another thing, an invading general should not have died so easily. His sword was expertly sharp, and she had the strength of those who see themselves as helpless. Using two hands, she even cut the pillow.

Judith's maid is running and has almost bumped into her. She is looking hard at her mistress' face. Her nose is slightly wrinkled; she is probably wondering if any blood from the basket on her head is leaking down into her hair. She thinks Judith is being theatrical. For some reason, perhaps to suggest motion, she has been drawn with only one leg. Where the other should be, there are just graceful folds of saffron cloth, but no outline of flesh. Unlike Judith, who is wearing delicate sandals, the maid has cloth boots, and is holding up her dress to keep it out of the dust. She feels like a hero, but wishes she were home.

XIX.
FEBRUARY 29

In front of the gold curtain
the sun has hung
the trees,
who are lost,
show me the way
pointing in all directions.

XX.
WILLIE

How come you dropped outa school?

I told him I ran out of money.

Lemme show you how to run
this here scaler.

Two whirling sets of chains
whipped the crust off the yellow-hot steel.

I wish I could go to college.
But when I got outa high school
I didn't wanna do nothing but
fuck around. So now I got 3 kids
and I gotta stay here.
But it ain't so bad. Something to do.

When the hammer's set up,
the line doesn't stop. Eight hours
we traded off shoving steel into the chains
dodging sparks big as dimes.

Wear a old shirt next time,
and a undershirt too.
I did like you did when I started off.
Really scarred up my chest.
See?
Kinda like stars.

x

XXI.
ROBES

1

She
just wanted
to
take a shower
He
followed
to see
her
yellow robe
drop

2

White
robe
She leaned
over the sink
looking
in the mirror
at her eyebrows
He
called her
a Martian
in her curlers

3

Vines
trellised the
bedroom walls
One white
candle
red robe
dark scented
oil

4

Her dog was
amused
at him
in her
green robe

5

Snow
up to the windows
In the
white light
of frost
she had
no robe at all